Change is Good You Go First

21 Ways to Inspire Change

MAC ANDERSON and TOM FELTENSTEIN

simple truths®
LEAD TO CHANGE

an imprint of Sourcebooks, Inc.

Photo Credits
Internals: page vii, Vector State; page 4, phipatbig/Shutterstock; page 8, Lynn Harker/Sourcebooks; page 12, 16, 22, 26, 30, Vector State; page 34, Lynn Harker/Sourcebooks; page 40, 52, 56–57, Vector State; page 58, Lynn Harker/Sourcebooks; page 68, Vector State; page 72, phipatbig/Shutterstock; page 76, Alvaro Cabrera Jimenez/Shutterstock, Vector State; page 80, 84, Vector State; page 88, phipatbig/Shutterstock; page 92, Vector Stock; page 100, Alexandr III/Shutterstock

Published by Simple Truths, an imprint of Sourcebooks, Inc.
P.O. Box 4410, Naperville, Illinois 60567-4410
(630) 961-3900
Fax: (630) 961-2168
www.sourcebooks.com

Printed and bound in the United States of America.
WOZ 10 9 8 7 6 5 4 3 2

Additional Simple Truths of Business

The Leadership Secrets of Santa Claus
Bull's-Eye
You Can't Send a Duck to Eagle School

CONTENTS

Introduction

Change is not easy. But it is simple. Things will always change. We don't have a choice about that, but we do have a choice on how we react to change; and as a leader whether or not we choose to create change. The choice really boils down to this…either we manage change, or it will manage us.

As a leader, however, deciding to make changes is the easy part. Getting your people on board is much more difficult. Why is that? Quite simply, change is an emotional process. We are all creatures of habit who usually resist it and welcome routine. Uncharted waters are scary!

In the long run, however, sameness is the fast track to mediocrity. And mediocre companies won't survive. Tuli Kupferberg said it best…"When patterns are broken, new worlds emerge." And that is your challenge…to convince your team that the new world you are trying to create is better than the one you're in. Is it easy? Of course not. It takes planning, commitment, patience, and courage.

The truth, of course, is that change can be a wonderful gift. In fact, it is the key that unlocks the doors to growth and excitement in any organization. And, most importantly, without it...your competition will pass you by. A big part of success, as a leader, will be your ability to inspire your team to get out of their comfort zones; to assure them that even though they are on a new path, it's the right path, for the right reasons.

That's what this book is all about...ideas, to inspire, to motivate, and to encourage your team to move forward and to embrace change. Our goal is simple...to help you reach yours.

Mac Anderson

Mac Anderson
Founder, Simple Truths and Successories

Tom Feltenstein

Tom Feltenstein
CEO, Power Marketing Academy

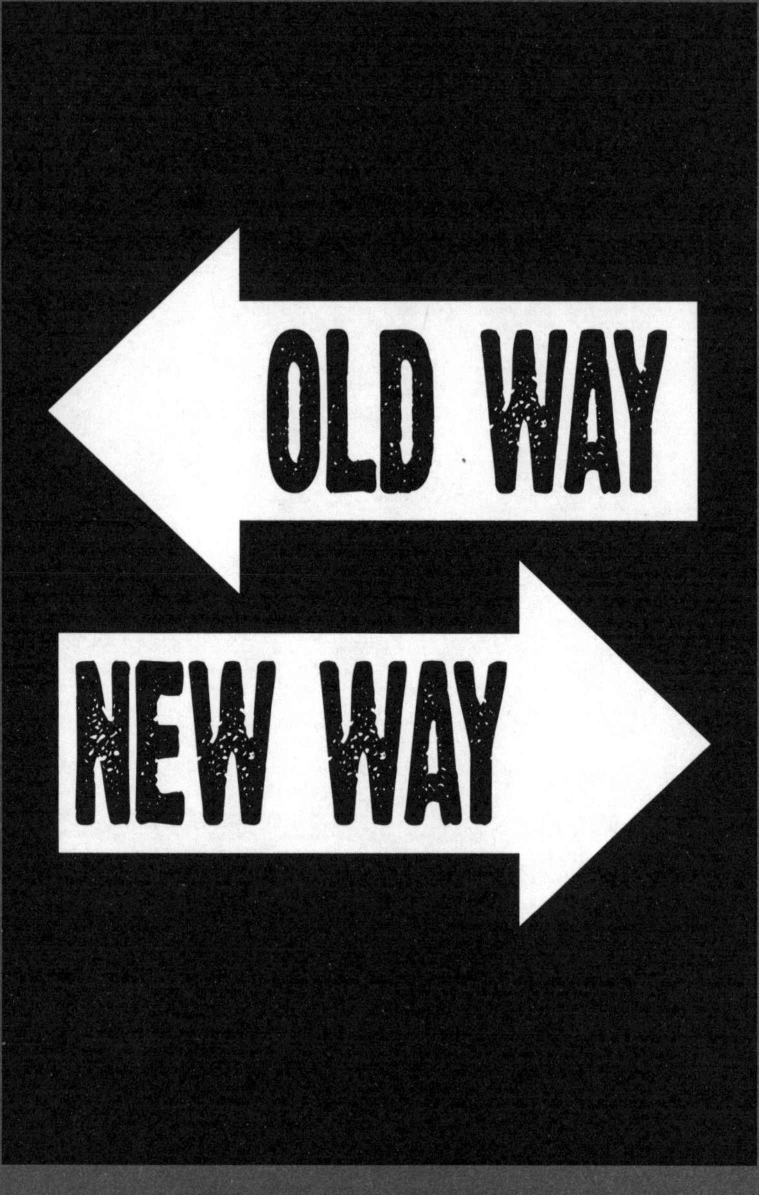
OLD WAY
NEW WAY

Change What Needs Changing... Not What's Easy

A few years ago, British Rail had a real falloff in business. Looking for marketing answers, they went searching for a new ad agency—one that could deliver an ad campaign that would bring their customers back.

When the British Rail executives went to the offices of a prominent London ad agency to discuss their needs, they were met by a very rude receptionist who insisted that they wait.

Finally, an unkempt person led them to a conference room—a dirty, scruffy room cluttered with plates of stale food. The executives were once again left to wait. A few agency people drifted in and out of the room, basically ignoring the executives who grew impatient by the minute. When the execs tried to ask what was going on, the agency people brushed them off and went about their work.

Eventually, the execs had enough. As they angrily started to get up, completely disgusted with the way they'd been treated, one of the agency people finally showed up.

"Gentlemen," he said, "your treatment here at our agency is not typical of how we treat our clients—in fact, we've gone out of our way to stage this meeting for you. We've behaved this way to point out to you what it's like to be a customer of British Rail. **Your real problem isn't your advertising, it's your people.** We suggest you let us address your employee attitude problem before we attempt to change your advertising."

The British Rail executives were shocked—but the agency got the account! The agency had the remarkable conviction to point out the problem because it knew exactly what needed to change.

As Yogi Berra once said:

Before we build a better mousetrap, we need to find out if there are any mice out there.

"If you don't like change, you're going to like irrelevance a lot less."

Tom Feltenstein

Re-Recruit Your Best People

As the old proverb goes, **"The journey of a thousand miles begins with a single step."** Your first step in the change process should be to re-recruit your best people. That of course starts with the managers of each department. Although the culture of any company starts at the top, it is the managers who will make it or break it, especially in times of change. Their attitude, their commitment, and understanding of the change mission will be key to your success.

Don't make the mistake of assuming they're on board, because it can be very costly and disruptive if you guess wrong. Even before the mission is clearly defined, bring them in, one on one, to get their input and their feedback. Get them involved in the planning process. But remember, there will be disagreements regarding your strategy and execution. And of course, that's where leadership comes into play.

In other words, if the manager disagrees with the final plan, you need to know up front. At this point, tough decisions must be made. They're either committed to the team's new plan going forward, or you need to find a new manager sooner rather than later.

Phase II of recruiting your best people will be up to each manager. Once you have mapped out a plan with each manager's input, you must toss the ball to them to have similar conversations with their best people. **A rule of thumb is this: out of every ten employees within a department, there is usually 1 that will have significant influence over how the others will think.** Each manager should identify those individuals and clearly communicate the changes that must be made. They must also explain the benefits to them and to the team. The manager must make these people a part of the change process and depend on each of them to help monitor the team's progress going forward. This investment of your time, and of each manager's time, will go a long way in helping to ensure your success.

"You get the best efforts from others not by **LIGHTING** a fire beneath them, but by **BUILDING** a fire within."

Bob Nelson

Forget for Success

Forget for Success is the title of a book written by Eric Harvey and Steve Ventura. In it they say, **"Our brains are like closets. Over time they are filled with things we no longer use—things that don't fit. Every once in a while they need to be cleaned out."**

How true it is! A big part of the change process is to be able to walk away from outdated beliefs and practices. But as we all know, old habits die hard. In fact, bestselling business author Peter Drucker said:

It's easier for companies to come up with new ideas than to let go of old ones.

Harvey and Ventura had this to say about cerebral baggage that weighs us down during change:

Our baggage includes everything from once valid beliefs and practices that have outlived their usefulness to misinformation and misconceptions that we've accepted (and even embraced) without much examination or thought.

Why care about this "baggage"? Because it negatively impacts us, the people we work with, the environment we work in, and the results we get. **Simply stated, whatever we accept and believe determines how we behave... and how we behave determines what we achieve (or don't achieve).**

Regardless of our good intentions, we're all susceptible to flawed thinking that eventually leads to flawed results. But if we dump this data from our memory banks, we free up space for more productive alternatives—we make room for the good stuff... **"the right stuff."**

"It's easier for companies to **COME UP WITH NEW IDEAS** than to let go of old ones."

Peter Drucker

It All Starts with Belief

At a speech I (Mac) gave recently, I was invited to attend the company's awards banquet the evening before. The previous year, the new CEO had thrown out a challenge for all six regions...whoever had the highest percent increase in revenue would get to host next year's annual meeting. Well, next year was here, and the winner was being honored.

After the CEO sang the winners' praises, the sales manager for the winning region stood up to say a few words, and here is what she said:

The day after last year's annual meeting, Peggy got us all together and told us, "Here are the rules for this year's contest, and by the way, we're going to win it! Why? Because we've got the best team!"

"Week after week she sold her vision of winning the contest; **she praised, she encouraged, she listened,** and within a few months, it hit home...**we all believed we could win it.**" The sales manager said, "It was a magical moment, going from I think we can win it, to I know we can win it." Then she said, **"We won for one reason... Peggy believed in us and believed we could do it...and we weren't about to let her down!"**

I have to tell you, I got goose bumps when I heard her speak about what had happened. This may sound trite to some leaders, but during times of change, **getting your team to believe it can be done is the most important thing you can do.** It won't happen overnight, but through continuous reinforcement, listening, encouragement, and most of all earning their trust, it will happen. And when it does, **a team becomes unstoppable!**

"A good leader inspires people to have confidence in their leader. A great leader **INSPIRES PEOPLE** to have **CONFIDENCE IN THEMSELVES.**"

Anonymous

Focus on Strengths

Changing customer tastes, nutritionally rooted lawsuits, globalization protests, and unprecedented brand erosion threatened to bring down the titanic of the corporate world. Triggered by its first ever quarterly loss since becoming a public company in 1965, were rumors of McDonald's demise exaggerated? **Could the company that turned marketing into an art form all of a sudden lose relevance?** It had gotten so bad that I (Tom) was invited to comment on national TV, and I stated what was obvious—they were spending fortunes on mass media and had lost customer focus.

CEO Jim Cantalupo was brought out of retirement to take over the helm. Along with him came teammates Charlie Bell (COO) and Larry Light (CMO), both seasoned veterans and close friends. Cantalupo announced that he would give himself eighteen months to turn the company around.

Sleeves rolled up, Light directed a worldwide research team to find the brand's strengths. "The first thing we began to notice was a commonality in five continents." He said, **"A fun, youthful spirit was at the core of the brand and our most dominant trait.** But we wanted to carefully distinguish between 'youthful spirit' and children. **Our brand is about attitude, not age."** They indoctrinated the "I'm lovin' it" attitude into all aspects of the company structure, including customer service, restaurant operations, menu food choices, and new restaurant décor.

In terms of the global responsibility, they stated "I don't think the question is whether or not it's fair or unfair; I think the question should be how do we make it an asset? We are a corporation that serves forty million customers a day. [McDonald's now serves sixty-nine million people every day.] Because of our size and scale, we have responsibilities. But I don't believe the solution is to grow smaller."

How did they pull it off? McDonald's changed its growth strategy from focusing on building more restaurants to attracting more customers to their existing restaurants.

McDonald's is now an intensely customer-focused company: **Listening, learning, and leading.** They implemented three corporate priorities—financial discipline, excellence in operations, and innovative marketing. McDonald's changed their fundamental operating structure. They defined the framework at the center, but fostered creative implementation locally. They reinvented global marketing and started gathering ideas from wherever they showed up. After all, a good idea doesn't care where it comes from. "I'm lovin' it" was born in Germany; global packaging was born in England; innovative restaurant designs were born in France.

Recently McDonald's extended its hot streak to four years with a 22 percent increase in first quarter earnings. The once stagnant stock quadrupled in less than four years. It set a record forty-eight straight months of higher sales from established restaurants, its longest streak since 1980.

CHANGE IS GOOD...YOU GO FIRST

So how does this apply to your organization? **The lesson to be learned from McDonald's is to focus first on your strengths, and make them all they can be.**

"FOCUS on the critical few, not the insignificant many."

Anonymous

Remove Barriers

If you're an employee, nothing is more frustrating than to understand the change mission, to embrace the change mission, but to be trapped by barriers beyond your control.

Job #1 for any leader in times of change is to start removing the barriers that will keep your team from executing the plan. For example, if the plan calls for creating a **"customer-first culture,"** you must identify any obstacles or barriers that will prevent you from doing it. Rest assured, however, that the culprits that are creating the obstacles will usually fall into one of four categories:

1. Outdated systems
2. Outdated procedures
3. Outdated people
4. A combination thereof

This, of course, assumes that your products are not part of the problem.

The first, and most important part of this challenge, is to do some serious diligence to **clearly define the "enemy."** This requires getting input from everyone, especially those frontline employees who are dealing directly with the customers. Your answers will come if you listen very carefully to what they have to say. Fixing what's broken, however, will take longer, especially if the finger is pointed at outdated systems. Fixing problems caused by outdated procedures and outdated people can take less time, but are just as critical to the change process.

In other words, the **obstacles to change will vary greatly.** They can be 20,000 pound boulders or they can be many small trees. **Your job as a leader is to start cutting the trees as quickly as you can so that the people watching will become convinced that good things are about to happen.**

"When you're up to your rear end in alligators, it's hard to remember that your purpose is draining the swamp."

George Napper

Simplify Your Message

After schooling in the States, the late Roberto Goizueta returned to Cuba in 1953 to work in his family's sugar business; but he was soon scanning want ads. He answered an anonymous ad for work at a Coca-Cola bottling plant in Cuba. There he would begin a famous career marked by his unique ability to inspire people.

In 1979, Goizueta was named the president of the Coca-Cola Company, and in 1981, the company's chairman. Over a sixteen-year span, Goizueta created more wealth for shareholders than any CEO in the company's history and made Coca-Cola the most prominent trademark in the world.

Though English was his third language, **his success is primarily attributed to his ability to encapsulate complex ideas and present them in concise,**

compelling fashion. Goizueta was best known for his oft-repeated description of Coca-Cola's infinite growth potential:

> *Each of the six billion people* [now seven billion] *on this planet drinks, on average, sixty-four ounces of fluids daily, of which only two ounces are Coca-Cola.*

Coca-Cola's employees were blown away by the originality and audacity of the idea when Goizueta first spoke it. **Eventually, closing the "sixty-two ounce gap" became a centerpiece of inspiration and motivation within the company.**

Nordstrom, the department store known for their great service has mastered the art of **"simplifying for success."** When it comes to taking care of the customer, they have only one rule for employees: "Use good judgment in all situations." One Nordstrom employee summed it up: **"Because we don't have many rules, we don't have to worry about breaking them. We are judged on our performance, not our obedience to orders."**

"Making the simple complicated is commonplace; making the complicated simple, awesomely simple— **THAT'S CREATIVITY.**"

Charles Mingus

Lead with Speed

In times of change there is always the question of…**How fast do we move?** Although there is no right answer for everyone, the right answer for most is…as fast as possible!

In John Kotter's book, *The Heart of Change,* he shares a story by Ron Marshall to reinforce the "how fast question." Marshall talked about how he bought his first house in New York. It was a sixty-five-year-old house…a real "fixer-upper," as he described it. At the closing, the realtor said, "Ron, you have to immediately make a list of all the things you want done and do it in the first six months." Marshall said, "I'm broke now but I'm a disciplined guy and I'll get everything fixed over the next few years." She said, "No, you won't, because after six months you'll get used to it. **You'll get used to stepping over the dead body in the living room.**"

Marshall then confessed, "She was right and I was

wrong. Nothing more had been done when I sold it five years later. The body was still there!"

This is exactly what can happen in the **"slow approach"** to change. **Inertia, if you don't act quickly, will stop you in your tracks.** You put out the fire, it feels a little better, and you continue to walk over the other "dead bodies" littered throughout the company. **Remember, on the road to lasting change, there will be many tempting places to pull over and park.**

Secondly, **speed is important in creating short-term wins.** Never underestimate the significance of early victories. They nourish the faith in the change effort, they give an emotional lift to those who are working hard, and they keep the cynics at bay. Also, and very importantly, each victory helps to build momentum, which can be a wonderful "friend" when you're riding the wave of change.

"Luck follows SPEED."

Darrel Royal

Let Your Customers Call the Shots

The only two-time recipient of the prestigious Malcolm Baldrige National Quality Award in the service category, the Ritz-Carlton Hotel Company, manages thirty-six exquisite hotels across the world. Known for their mystical aura of customer service, they also have challenges when it comes to change.

A few years back, they decided to upgrade the bathrooms in their signature properties. They insisted on the best and most beautiful décor. The company invested millions of dollars in design fees, they hand-selected the precise hue, color, and pattern of their green marble imported from Italy. After spending millions of dollars and shipping tons of the most exquisite marble across the world, they installed it meticulously in their guest bathrooms.

After all this expense and effort, the company commissioned a research study to ask its customers questions about its service, accommodations, and ambience. **The results were shocking to the Ritz-Carlton executives.** Guests couldn't care less about green marble in their bathrooms; they wanted the bathrooms to be pure white, so they could see it was clean. Their efforts, time, and money had gone completely by the wayside.

Bouncing back, management took specific actions to capitalize on the other opportunities for improvement. It revamped its strategic planning process and made it more systematic. It refined and integrated its total quality management. **Goals for customer satisfaction were raised to the "top of the box."** Earning a rating of "very" or "extremely" satisfied became a top priority as well as a key element of the Ritz-Carlton strategy—100 percent customer loyalty. In its operations, the company set the target of "error-free" experiences for guests and implemented a quantitative measurement system to chart the progressive elimination of even the most minute customer problems.

Steps for quality improvement and problem-solving procedures were identified, analyzed, and accounted for. For example, they documented and planned for 970 potential problem instances during interactions with overnight guests and 1,071 such instances with event planners.

Every day at every Ritz-Carlton, employees from every department worldwide, gather for a fifteen minute meeting called "the lineup," where they review guest experiences, resolve issues, and discuss ways to improve service. **The meetings revolve around the heroic performance of a Ritz-Carlton employee known as the "wow story."**

Carmine Gallo writes about a family staying at the Ritz-Carlton Bali, who carried special eggs and milk for their son who suffered from food allergies. Upon arrival, the concierge saw that the eggs had broken and the milk had soured. The manager and dining staff searched the town but could not find the items. The executive chef at the resort remembered a store in Singapore that sold them. He contacted his mother-in-law and asked that she buy the products and fly to Bali to deliver them at once. The family was delighted. Because of the Ritz-Carlton's impeccable system the story was instantly circulated around the world to inspire, teach, and remind the 36,000 employees worldwide of its commitment to flawless service.

Change is only appreciated if it is meaningful or appreciated in the eyes of the beholder. Are your communications, your actions of relevance to your customer? If they aren't, you too, could end up under a whole heap of green marble.

"Success doesn't happen by accident. It starts with an unwavering commitment to build a dedicated team who serves their boss…
THE CUSTOMER."

Mac Anderson

Let Your Actions Speak

"You can't teach culture. **You have to live it. You have to experience it. You have to share it. You have to show it.**" These are words from Brent Harris, a top executive for Nordstrom, the retail chain known for legendary service.

To change any culture, in any company, the people at the top have to show it! Because words without deeds mean nothing.

When David Neeleman started the airline Jet Blue, he knew the importance of leading from the front and letting his actions speak. His mission was to create a customer service culture, and he knew all eyes would be watching.

Not long ago, I read a great story in *Inc.* magazine written by Norm Brodsky. In it, Brodsky wrote about being on a Jet Blue flight when Neeleman was on board…

"As we were buckling up to take off, Neeleman stood up and introduced himself. 'Hi, I'm Dave Neeleman, the CEO of Jet Blue. I'm here to serve you today and I'm looking forward to meeting every one of you before we land.'

"As he was handing out snack baskets he would stop to chat with everyone. When he came to me, I told him I thought it was a great idea to serve his customer firsthand, and asked him how often he did it. Expecting him to say once or twice a year, he said, **'Not often enough...I get to do it about once a month.'**

"Out of curiosity, I watched him interact with other passengers. In several instances, I saw him taking notes and listening intently to what passengers were saying. In a few instances when he couldn't answer the question, I watched him take a business card and say, 'Someone will be in touch with you in the next twenty-four hours.' Even at the end of the flight, there was Neeleman, in his blue apron, leading the charge collecting the trash from the seat pockets."

Now, here's a question for you… **Is there any doubt that Jet Blue employees knew that their leader was willing to walk the talk when it came to serving the customers? And, is there any doubt that the front line knew he was on their team?**

When asked if he thought leading by example was the most important quality of leadership, the great humanitarian Albert Schweitzer thought for a second, and then replied, *"No, it's not the most important one. It's the only one."*

"NOTHING IS SO CONTAGIOUS AS AN EXAMPLE. We never do great good or

great evil without bringing about more of the same on the part of others."

François de La Rochefoucauld

PERSONAL
RESPONSIBILITY
IN
DELIVERING
EXCELLENCE

Inspire Personal Accountability

Something magic happens when we accept personal responsibility for our behavior and our results. But it's not easy, because it's human nature to "pass the buck." I (Mac) know there have been times in my life when my business was struggling where I found myself blaming others, blaming the economy, blaming this, blaming that! But as I've gotten older (and a little wiser) **when things go wrong in my business, or my life, I can always find the culprit...in the mirror.** In every instance, it always comes back to choices I've made in my life that put me exactly where I am today. **I have to say that this one "tweak" in my attitude may sound like a little thing, but it has made a big difference in my life.**

What does all this have to do with change? Plenty! As a manager, one of the most important things you can do in times of change is to get your people to understand how their taking personal responsibility, their recognizing problems as opportunities, will not only help the company, but will help them as individuals. **In other words, sell the idea of...what's in it for them?**

Authors B.J. Gallagher and Steve Ventura wrote a great little book about achieving success through personal accountability titled *Who Are "They" Anyway?* I like their list showing how each individual in the company can benefit by adopting a "personal accountability attitude":

- You have more control over your destiny.

- You become an active contributor rather than a passive observer.

- Others look to you for leadership.

- You gain the reputation as a problem solver.

- You enhance your career opportunities.

- You enjoy the satisfaction that comes from getting things done...the power of positive doing.

- You experience less anger, frustration, and helplessness—all leading to better physical health.

- You realize a positive spillover effect into your personal life at home.

According to Gallagher and Ventura, the most important words of personal responsibility are as follows:

The 10 most important words:
I won't wait for others to take the first step.

The 9 most important words:
If it is to be, it's up to me.

The 8 most important words:
If not me, who? If not now, when?

The 7 most important words:
Let me take a shot at it.

The 6 most important words:
I will not pass the buck.

The 5 most important words:
You can count on me.

The 4 most important words:
It IS my job!

The 3 most important words:
Just do it!

The 2 most important words:
I will.

The most important word:
Me

Frank Tyger said it best: *"Your future depends on many things, but most yourself."*

"I always wondered why somebody didn't do something about that.

Then I realized I WAS SOMEBODY."

Lily Tomlin, Comedienne, Actress, and Author

Celebrate Success

A paycheck is what an employee works for. Recognition and praise is what they live for! **Every manager should understand that recognition is a human need...one that we all crave.** And one of your greatest challenges is to find creative ways to fill that need. **Many times this one thing can be the difference between a good and a great leader.** Michael LeBoeuf understood this when he said, **"The greatest management principle in the world is 'the things that get rewarded and appreciated get done.'"**

During the change process, an effective recognition practice is to celebrate successes, and to reinforce your goals on a daily, weekly, and monthly basis. **You are making an investment in your most important asset: your people!**

When creating a recognition program, think about these three main categories:

1. **Formal awards:** These are rewards that are predetermined by management, where employees are formally recognized for their outstanding efforts. They are usually presented in front of the recipient's peers on a monthly, quarterly, or yearly basis.

   Examples of these awards include:

   > ***Employee of the Month***
   > ***President's Club Award***
   > ***Extra Mile Award***

   In most cases, organizations will offer personalized awards, such as plaques or engraved crystal. However, sometimes, depending on the significance of the award, other gifts can be given (i.e., trips, watches, a day off, cash).

2. **Informal awards:** Informal award programs are designed to recognize people who have met specific goals. **This is immediate recognition given by managers to someone doing something right.** They are meant to be symbolic and memorable...not costly. Examples of informal awards can be a departmental celebration, a free lunch, a gift certificate, a coffee mug, and of course...gift books to inspire and to reinforce your company's values!

3. **Day-to-day awards:** Day-to-day awards are **simple acts of kindness, gratitude,** and **respect**. They come in the form of written thank-you notes, letters of appreciation, or positive feedback via voice mail or email. These awards play a very important role in employee satisfaction and loyalty. Tom Peters so wisely said, "We wildly underestimate the power of the tiniest personal touch."

Never forget...recognition is a need we all crave. It creates heart power, and in times of change, heart power is more important than ever.

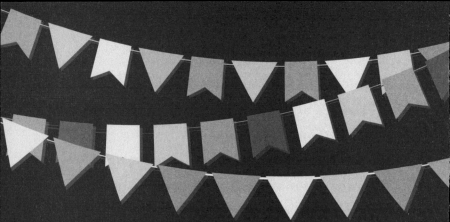

"Compensation is a right,

RECOGNITION
IS A GIFT."

Rosabeth Kanter

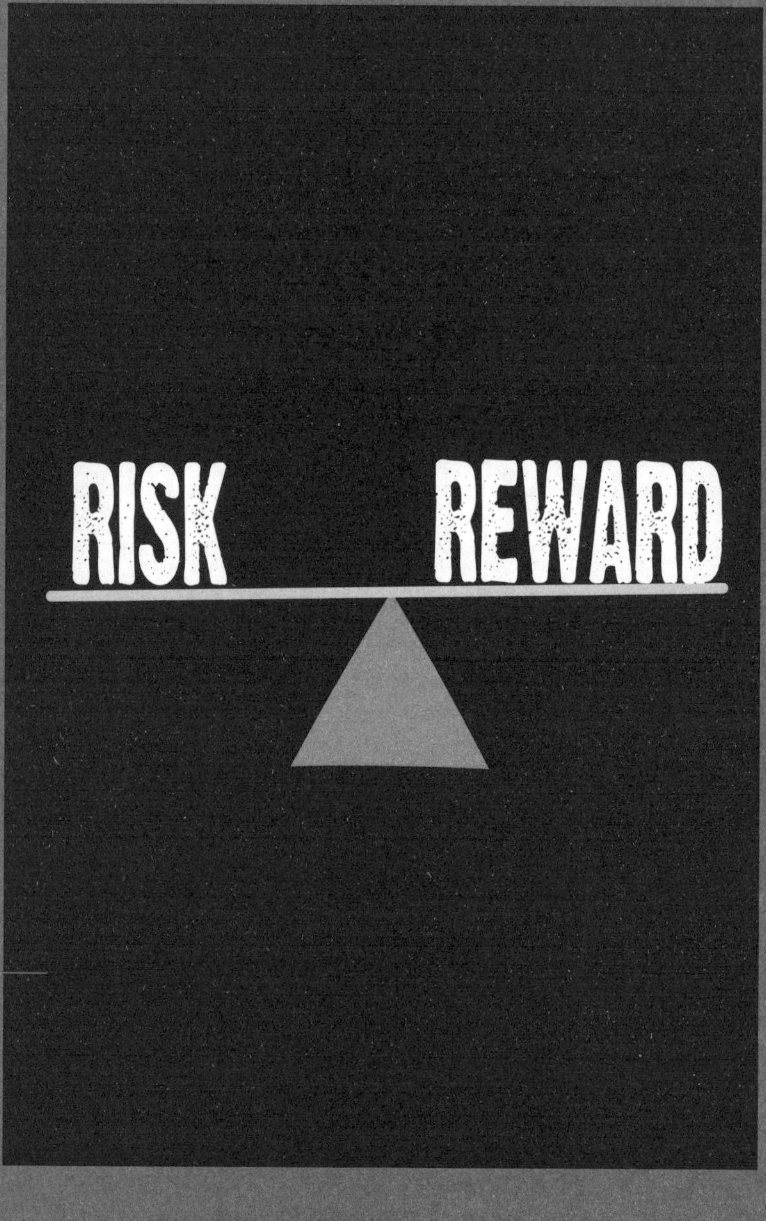
RISK
REWARD

Take Calculated Risks

In a bold move featured on the front page of the *Wall Street Journal*, Brad Anderson, CEO of Best Buy, America's number one electronics retailer, decided to fire 20 percent of his customers by eliminating specific promotions and sales tactics. **This action showed a conviction and an unwillingness to live with the status quo that exemplifies the character of true leaders.**

After analyzing the purchase histories of customer groups, Anderson discovered that 20 percent of his customers were responsible for virtually all the transactions in which the company lost money, while an entirely different 20 percent accounted for the bulk of store profits. To prepare for the change, Anderson trained his "on the floor sales staff" in 100 pilot stores. He got them to quickly recognize and accommodate their high-profit customers.

Surprisingly, price was not the issue to this group of customers, yet they were responsible for most of the revenue in the company; hence, the importance of recognizing your customer's value.

He changed the way his salespeople talked to these high-end customers. He trained them to describe the benefits of their products and to upsell them on additional features, warranties, and options in a way that this highly targeted group would appreciate. At the same time, **he eliminated all discounting and price driven promotions to deter the 20 percent of customers that resulted in unprofitable transactions.** Within a few months, Best Buy's 100 pilot stores posted double the sales gains of the other stores. Promptly, the change was exported to the remaining stores with great success.

When viewed after the fact, change appears to follow a specific—almost predetermined—path. Numbers and probabilities are just educated opinions of the past; they are not a future guarantee.

In retrospect, the challenge, the fear, the hesitation involved in firing 20 percent of his customers wasn't even mentioned in the article. Our story portrays a logical, factual, timely, orderly progression of facts and events. Yet we all know that any story worth its salt has an element of the unknown, an element of change and a sprinkling of risk. **Anderson had no guarantee his strategy would work, but his courage to try it paid off.**

"PROGRESS INVOLVES RISK...

You can't steal second base and keep your foot on first."

Frederick Wilcox

TOGETHER

EVERYONE

ACHIEVES

MORE

Learn from "Old Warwick"

Fostering a spirit of teamwork is critical in times of change. The key element is trust. Trust for the leader and trust for each other.

There is a wonderful story from the play, *Some Folks Feel the Rain; Others Just Get Wet*, that I (Mac) shared in my book, *You Can't Send a Duck to Eagle School*. And I think it's worth sharing again to shed some light on how people think about working together:

> *A man was lost while driving through the country. As he tried to reach for the map, he accidentally drove off the road into a ditch. Though he wasn't injured, his car was stuck deep in the mud. So the man walked to a nearby farm to ask for help.*
>
> *"Warwick can get you out of that ditch," said the farmer, pointing to an old mule standing in a field.*

The man looked at the decrepit old mule and looked at the farmer who just stood there repeating, "Yep, old Warwick can do the job." The man figured he had nothing to lose. The two men and the mule made their way back to the ditch. The farmer hitched the mule to the car. With a snap of the reins, he shouted, "Pull, Fred! Pull, Jack! Pull, Ted! Pull, Warwick!"

And the mule pulled that car right out of the ditch.

The man was amazed. He thanked the farmer, patted the mule, and asked, "Why did you call out all of those names before you called Warwick?"

The farmer grinned and said, "Old Warwick is just about blind. As long as he believes he's part of a team, he doesn't mind pulling."

"TEAMWORK is the ability to work together toward a common vision. The ability to direct individual accomplishment toward organizational objectives. **IT IS THE FUEL THAT ALLOWS COMMON PEOPLE TO OBTAIN UNCOMMON RESULTS."**

SUCCESSORIES® Print

Respect the Growing Process

Like the gardener, *the effective leader recognizes that change takes time to take root.* And pulling up the "roots" before the process has matured is a sure way to confuse people, and destroy what has been started. There is a story about a Japanese executive who stressed the need for patience and discipline when it comes to quality. "Sometimes," he said, "the quality process is like farming bamboo. Once the bamboo seed is planted the farmer waters it every day. He does that for four years before the tree even breaks ground. But, when it finally does, it grows sixty feet in the next ninety days." **This story reminds us that change, like quality, will need time to "take root" before the full benefits are realized.**

Along the way, however, there will be many challenges. Most leaders know that there are no shortcuts to any place worth going. **In times of change we**

must remember...mistakes will be made. We must remember that people will be people.

We differ. We have doubts. We assume too much. This is where great teams outshine the rest. They see differences as advantages, not excuses to give up. They understand that patience and perseverance are great virtues, and the mark of wisdom and strength. *So plant the right seeds, respect the growing process, and watch great things happen!*

"Patience is bitter, but the fruit can BE SWEET."

Benjamin Franklin

Measure Results

Most employees want to grow, they want to do better, they want to take pride in their work, but they need targets to shoot for. **Unless they have clearly defined goals, the "path of least resistance" will almost always raise its ugly head.**

In the words of Peter Drucker, **"What we measure gets improved."** Of course, Drucker's quote is true for any business any time; however, during change it is even more critical.

Let's circle back to the example of a company attempting to create a "customer-first culture." Now, let's ask yourself the question...**what activities can I measure to track our progress in this situation?** First, of course, you must determine where you are now with each activity you wish to improve. Secondly, you need to set realistic targets for improvement. Thirdly, and most importantly, you must track, monitor, and review results on a daily, weekly, and monthly basis. Now this may sound boring, but it is critical to break old habits and to inspire new thinking.

Here are just a few examples on what could be measured to track your progress:

- What percentage of phone calls are being answered on the first, second, or third ring?

- What percentage of orders are being processed, and shipped, on the same day, the second day, or the third day?

- What percentage of orders have products that are back ordered?

In your customer satisfaction surveys, **what percentage of your customers are giving your service an excellent rating, a good rating, a fair rating, etc.?**

The answers to all of these questions will give you the answer to that question which everyone is looking for in times of change...

Are we making progress toward our goal?

"What gets measured GETS IMPROVED."

Peter Drucker

Set the Stage
for Innovation

Linus Pauling said, **"The best way to get a good idea is to get lots of ideas." Not rocket science, but it works!** The only way to keep a change culture alive, long-term, is to set the stage for innovation. Kevin Kelly, in his book, *New Rules for the New Economy*, said:

> *Wealth today flows directly from innovation, not optimization. It is not gained by perfecting the know, but by imperfectly seizing the unknown.*

Tomorrow comes at us with lightning speed, and your competitive advantage is a fleeting thing. As leaders, we must create an environment that puts innovation front and center. Your people must know it is the key to your company's survival. **You must create a climate that rewards risk and creative effort.** Your people must not fear mistakes, but understand that honest mistakes can be life's main source for learning. **So teach them to fail quickly and often to enable them to reach the next plateau.**

Far too many leaders consider innovation the business equivalent of football's Hail Mary pass or the buzzer-beating three-pointer in basketball. On rare occasions it might work, but "rare occasions," and "might work" are not the foundation of effective innovation programs. **Innovation requires a system, a culture, leadership, and an allocation of resources.** Then it becomes a matter of discipline, commitment, and determination.

Tom Peters gets it. He said:

I've spent a good part of my life studying economic successes and failures. Above all, I've learned that everything takes a back seat to innovation.

"WE KEEP MOVING FORWARD, opening new doors, and doing new things. Our curiosity keeps **TAKING US DOWN NEW PATHS."**

Walt Disney

Inspire with Stories

A friend of University of Tennessee coach Phillip Fulmer once sent him a hand-carved walking stick. It arrived at the school about the time the coach was heading out to practice. He took it with him to show the players. **"Gosh, Coach," they said, "you look like Moses."** Fulmer took it as a jab at his aging body and graying hair, so he gave the stick to the equipment manager and had him store it in his office.

Then that night, it hit him. Moses wasn't just some gray-haired, bent over, old guy. He led the people to the Promised Land.

The next day, he took the stick back out to practice and put the team in a circle. "Okay," he said, "yesterday you guys said I looked like Moses with this thing, right?" He then reminded them of the story of Moses and the Israelites and explained how the stick was going to be the focal point of their energy. They couldn't tell their girlfriends, their families, or the media about it, **but they would take the stick wherever they went and it would be a reminder of what they had to do to reach their Promised Land.**

The team bought into it. The stick was passed around to different team leaders and each became responsible for bringing it to the practices and meetings. When the team traveled to games, the players would ask, "Hey Coach, you got the stick?" At every game, it stood on the sideline, a constant reminder of the greater story unfolding with every play.

A trip to the Promised Land wasn't just a creative gimmick; it was Coach Fulmer's way of inviting the young men into a great story, an epic bigger than their individual lives. **The walking stick wasn't the source of their motivation. It was a visual reminder of the larger story they were writing. In every meeting, at every practice, and throughout every game.** This all took place in 1998, the year the Tennessee Volunteers crossed over into the NCAA Promised Land by **winning their first consensus National Championship since 1954.**

Each of us wants to be part of something bigger than ourselves. Call it purpose, destiny, or a simple desire to get beyond the insufficiencies of our current existence. An individual's yearning to reach outside his life is a seed of greatness waiting for a stream of inspiration. Carving that stream into people's hearts is a simpler task if the endeavor you are leading them into is attached to a bigger story.

"A storyteller, like a travel agent, can help gather us up from wherever we are, and put us down in another setting."

John Leggett

Follow Your Convictions

They'd been a client of mine (Tom) for seven consecutive years. Every year they had increased sales, and the company opened many new locations. I was meeting with their top executives, brilliant people doing what they do best. Yet that Tuesday afternoon years of trust and success flew out the door as my recommendation landed like a ton of bricks. What ensued wasn't resistance; it was a battle. My prior experience in dealing with corporate bureaucracy of top companies did nothing to prepare me for what was to come.

I suggested they give away their signature entrée—a three-pound lobster dinner—as a gift to their patrons on the day of their birthday. At first they chuckled and laughed, and then the room became silent. I told them I was serious and proceeded to explain the details of the promotion. The silence turned to anger and anger turned to outrage as I explained the points to no avail. The CFO asked me if I was nuts, threw his hands up in the air and pounded the table in disgust. The tension grew out of proportion—the president asked me to leave the room and return only when I'd come to my senses.

I left the meeting and headed for the park. I sat on a bench and contemplated his point. After all, the promotion would shoot down healthy revenues from this high-yielding entrée. I spent hours walking the park. Later that afternoon, I walked back into the office and told the president I'd come to my senses and there'd be no way I would retract my recommendation. **I would stay until everyone was convinced and the entire program was perfectly laid out.**

It took seven hours of intense selling, arguing, discussing, rebutting, and listening—but never giving an inch. It was midnight when all of us left the room. I don't think it was my eloquence; I just wore them down until they surrendered from exhaustion. The promotion would run.

Now, twelve years later, it's still the most profitable promotion with an unprecedented 50 percent redemption rate and a healthy stream of millions of extra revenue. The promotion was single-handedly responsible for a 7 percent same-store sales boost during the first year alone.

I knew that not one of their wealthy patrons would dine alone on their birthday, so the thought of a loss was out of the question. That an outrageous gift—like a three pound lobster (instead of a sirloin) would generate excitement, commotion, and word of mouth. Most importantly, that the birthday person would invite three or more of their best friends and relatives to dine with them and share this experience.

"They focused on what was—I saw what could be. But together, we made it happen."

In times of change, when you know something is right, you must follow your convictions. Keep going until you make the change—and most importantly—expect great resistance along the way.

Stand with Them, Not above Them

In the summer of 1941, Sergeant James Allen Ward was awarded the Victoria Cross for climbing onto the wing of his Wellington bomber, 13,000 feet above the North Sea, to extinguish a fire in the starboard engine. Secured only by a rope around his waist, he not only smothered the fire but shimmied along the wing back to the cabin.

Not long after, Winston Churchill, an admirer of courageous acts, summoned the shy New Zealander to 10 Downing Street.

Sergeant Ward was struck dumb in Churchill's presence and unable to answer the prime minister's questions. Churchill noted the hero's condition.

"You must feel very humble and awkward in my presence," Churchill said.

"Yes, sir," managed Ward.

"Then you can imagine," replied Churchill, "how humble and awkward I feel in yours."

Great leaders know that positive change requires a secure measure of buy-in with followers. And the greater the change, the greater the buy-in must be.

You don't have to be a good leader to get people to follow you on an unchanging course. You can be an average leader and some will still follow you through minor bends in the road. **But to get people to follow you through the unpredictable twists and turns, you must not only sell your vision, you must show that you care.** Humility is a powerful trait that all great leaders possess. Ben Franklin understood. He said, *"To be humble to superiors is duty, to equals courtesy, to inferiors nobleness."*

"The measure of a **TRULY GREAT MAN** is the courtesy with which he treats lesser men."

Anonymous

Pull the Weeds

It's one thing to be loyal; it's another to be dumb. Looking back on my (Mac) career as an entrepreneur, there were a number of times I was loyal to a fault. My instincts told me a person was not right for the job but my heart urged me to give them one more chance. In thirty years of business, dwindling confidence in an employee never improved by waiting. **I've learned it is better to hire slowly to secure the right person, and fire quickly when your gut says you made a mistake.** Or, as John Murphy says in his book, *Pulling Together*, leaders must learn to "pull the weeds."

"Life is full of choices," writes Murphy. **"Some people will choose to work for the team and embrace your culture. Others will not."** It's a reality an outgoing leader finds hard to bear. Some people won't like where you're leading them; others might not like you.

CHANGE IS GOOD...YOU GO FIRST

Like it or not, leaders must continually "pull the weeds" or their team's growth will be stifled. **A "weed" makes its own rules, undermining camaraderie and consensus.** They refuse to share and participate. They reject accountability and shift blame to others. Don't be fooled. "Weeds" can seem harmless...but, they'll do everything they can to take over your garden.

For years, Jack Welch had a rule that his managers must develop criteria to measure the performance of all employees. They were instructed to identify the bottom ten percent in each department and replace them with "new blood." His controversial rule caused some problems for GE and was eventually eliminated in the name of political correctness, but it's hard to argue with the company's long-term success. I disagree with tying employment to a percentage, but I agree that new faces and fresh ideas can improve a company, especially when they are supplanting weeds. *In the long run, if a leader keeps to the path of least resistance and lets weeds grow, they will risk losing credibility with those who make the team flourish.*

"**LEADERSHIP**
would be easy
if it wasn't
for people."

REINFORCE

REINFORCE

REINFORCE

Reinforce, Reinforce, Reinforce

I'm sure you've heard the three keys to purchasing real estate… location, location, location. Well you'll now hear the three keys to inspiring change…**reinforce, reinforce, reinforce.** Many leaders in times of change grossly underestimate the need for continuous reinforcement. **In a perfect world we hear something once, record it in our brain, and never need to hear it again. But in reality, our worlds are far from perfect.** During a time of change we have doubts, fears, and occasional disappointments. Sometimes there are friends, family, and coworkers reinforcing those doubts saying, "It won't work."

Once the management team has signed off on the "change message," the challenge is how do you keep it alive until the behavior is consistent with your goals.

CHANGE IS GOOD...YOU GO FIRST

Understand one thing...it won't happen on its own. You need to have a plan in place to make it happen. Answering these three questions is a first step for success:

1. How do I keep it simple? Less is always more.
2. How can I make it memorable?
3. How many times can I communicate it, on a daily, weekly, and monthly basis?

To some this may sound like simple, commonsense stuff. But to do it right, it's anything but simple. It takes creative planning and input from everyone involved. **But, most of all, it takes tremendous discipline to keep the "train on the track."** A lot of little things will make a big difference in convincing the team that you're 100 percent committed to making change happen. So sweat the small stuff and remember...**reinforce, reinforce, reinforce.**

"When patterns
are broken,
**NEW
WORLDS
EMERGE.**"

Tuli Kupferberg

About the
AUTHORS

Tom Feltenstein

Tom Feltenstein began his career with McDonald's, rising up to become a senior-level executive under the tutelage of Ray Kroc—McDonald's legendary founder.

As founder of the Neighborhood Marketing Institute, and CEO of Power Marketing Academy, Tom has consulted with more than 500 businesses, yet he's the best kept secret—outside of the corporate arena. Tom has received acclaim from the media for the uncommon wisdom he shared on the *Larry King Show*, traded barbs on the *David Letterman Show*, and argued the waste of running ads during the Super Bowl on Fox News Pre-Game Show.

A sought-after speaker, well-known coach, trainer, and strategist, Tom's also a widely published author. He has written fourteen books, including *Uncommon Wisdom: Live a Joyful Life with Financial Success* (2003); *Marketing, the Good, the Bad, the Ugly: Success, Failure and the Sure Thing* (2014); and *501 Killer Marketing Tactics to Increase Sales, Maximize Profits, and Stomp Your Competition* (2010).

For more information please visit www.tomfeltenstein.com or call (561) 650-1315.

Mac Anderson

Mac Anderson is the founder of Simple Truths and Successories, Inc., the leader in designing and marketing products for motivation and recognition. These companies, however, are not the first success stories for Mac. He was also the founder and CEO of McCord Travel, the largest travel company in the Midwest, and part owner/VP of Sales for Orval Kent Food Company, the country's largest manufacturer of prepared salads. Mac's accomplishments in these unrelated industries provide some insight into his passion and leadership skills.

Mac brings the same passion to his speaking and writing. He speaks to many corporate audiences on a variety of topics, including leadership, motivation, and team building.

He has written many books, including: *You Can't Send a Duck to Eagle School*, *The Nature of Success*, *The Power of Attitude*, and *The Essence of Leadership*, and has coauthored *To a Child*, *Love Is Spelled T-I-M-E*, *The Dash*, and *212° The Extra Degree*.

For more information, please visit www.simpletruths.com or call (800) 900-3427.